THE BUCKET LIST GUIDE TO LIFE SKILLS

BY STEPHANIE PETERS

CAPSTONE PRESS
a capstone imprint

Published by Capstone Press, an imprint of Capstone
1710 Roe Crest Drive, North Mankato, Minnesota 56003
capstonepub.com

Library of Congress Cataloging-in-Publication Data is available on the Library of Congress website.

ISBN: 9781669003816 (hardcover)
ISBN: 9781669003779 (ebook PDF)

Summary: How do you make it through life and accomplish everything you want? With a bucket list, of course! Learn how to speak up and be heard, balance money, spread your wings, and more in this easy-to-follow guide guaranteed to help you tackle all the items on your life skills bucket list.

Editor: Donald Lemke; Designer: Kay Fraser;
Media Researcher: Svetlana Zhurkin;
Production Specialist: Katy LaVigne

Image Credits
Getty Images: ajkkafe, cover (bottom right), Alistair Berg, 8, Alys Tomlinson, 14, gahsoon, 27, JGI/Jamie Grill, 15, Jose Luis Pelaez Inc, 6, 12, 24, 26, Lucy Lambriex, 29, Maskot, 17, PhotoAlto/Eric Audras, 16, RF Pictures, 21, SDI Productions, 25; Shutterstock: Inside Creative House, 10, Monkey Business Images, cover (bottom left), 4, 7, 18, 22, New Africa, 23, otnaydur, 9, pixelheadphoto digitalskillet, 19, Plateresca, 28, Prostock-studio, cover (right), Sergey Novikov, 20, silverkblackstock, 11, Suzanne Tucker, 13, Tatiana Gladskikh, 5

All internet sites appearing in back matter were available and accurate when this book was sent to press.

Printed and bound in the USA. 5195

CONTENTS

Words in **bold** appear in the glossary.

LEARNING LIFE SKILLS

Life skills can help you tackle everyday challenges head-on. These skills also make great bucket list items.

Ready to start? The advice in this book will guide you toward creating your best life skills bucket list!

SPEAK UP AND BE HEARD

You use your voice to talk. But are you using it to **communicate**? Good communication is key to getting along with others. It's a skill worth working on!

CAN I SAY SOMETHING?

Who's taking out the trash? Where are we going on vacation? Families make decisions like these every day. Your opinion matters. Add your voice to the **conversation**! Making sure you are heard is a skill for life.

LEAD ON

Being a leader is an important life skill and bucket list item. Group activities often go better with someone in charge. A good leader **inspires** a group to do its best. They **motivate** group members toward a goal.

MAY I HAVE YOUR ATTENTION, PLEASE?

Do you get **stage fright** at the thought of giving a speech? You're not alone. Public speaking scares a lot of people. Finding the confidence to address a crowd is a useful life skill.

FACT: The fear of public speaking is called glossophobia.

MONEY SMARTS

Money is part of our lives. Knowing how to handle your own money is a bucket list life skill everyone can use!

MAKE SOME

Buying the things we need or want takes money. If there's something special you want, you could ask an adult to pay for it. Or you could earn the money yourself!

Making money is an important skill. It's also rewarding, especially if you earn it doing something you like.

SAVE SOME

Spending money is fun. But it's good to get in the **habit** of saving too. That way, you'll have cash for big-ticket items, like a visit to an amusement park. Putting money aside to spend later is a life skill you'll be glad you mastered.

ACTIVITY: MONEY JARS

Want to see your savings grow? Plant your earnings in money jars. Find glass or plastic containers. (Recycled spaghetti sauce jars work well!) Label the jars *pennies*, *nickels*, *dimes*, *quarters*, and *dollars*. If you're saving up for something specific, add another label with that item's name on it. Keep adding to the jars. In time, your savings will bloom!

BORROW AND LEND

At some point, you might need to **borrow** money from someone. Make sure you both agree that the money will be paid back. Decide when the payback will happen. That way, you'll both feel OK with the **loan**. You'll also gain experience handling money.

TAKE CARE, NOW

When you were little, your parents or other adults took care of you. Now that you're older, you can start taking care of yourself and those around you. Learning responsibility can be a great addition to any bucket list.

GIVE YOURSELF A BREAK

With school, homework, and **extracurricular** activities, life can get busy. It's easy to feel **overwhelmed**. If that happens, talk to an adult. Together, you can figure out how to take breaks when needed.

SHARE IN THE CARE

Taking care of a pet, plant, or younger sibling is a long-lasting skill. It shows others that you're trustworthy and kind. It also proves that the well-being of others is important to you.

SPREAD YOUR WINGS

The older you get, the more chances you'll have to explore your place in the world. Understanding your interests can help shape your life journey.

YOU WON'T KNOW UNTIL YOU TRY!

New activities can be scary. It can be easy to steer clear of something if you think you won't be any good at it. But no one starts out perfect at anything! Accepting that you'll make mistakes is a valuable life skill.

SOMEONE ELSE'S SHOES

People from all walks of life face difficulties every day. No one person can fix every problem. But you can take steps to make a positive impact. Getting involved with giving back is a life skill worth adding to your bucket list.

ACTIVITY: DONATION DRIVE

Do you have a cause you want to support? Consider holding a donation drive, where people donate items to be sold. All money raised goes toward the cause. It takes time and energy to organize a drive, so be sure you have plenty of both.

FACT:

Charity is an emotional response to give money for an immediate need. Philanthropy raises money to address ongoing needs.

A PROBLEM? NO PROBLEM!

Someday, you'll have your first job. Many employers look for people who can think on their feet to solve problems. You can practice that life skill now. Then you'll be ready when job opportunities come your way!

WANT TO TRY MORE?

You've got all the important life skills bucket list items! Now it's time to add some fun activities and experiences to your must-do list. Check out (and then check off) a few of these ideas.

- ☑ Ask an adult to teach you how to do your own laundry.
- ☑ Learn yoga poses by taking a class or following online instruction.
- ☑ Make your own soap by melting chopped-up blocks of glycerin in the microwave. Mix in colored dye and fragrance oils, pour the mixture into molds, and chill until hardened.

- ☑ Play the sticky note game with friends and family. Ask yes-or-no questions to guess the person, place, or thing written on the note stuck to your forehead.
- ☑ Create cheerful greeting cards to give to random people.
- ☑ Volunteer to stock and bag items at your local food pantry.
- ☑ Interview adults to learn more about their jobs.
- ☑ Help out with a youth sports team.

GLOSSARY

borrow (BOR-oh)—to use something that belongs to someone else, with permission

communicate (kuh-MYOO-nuh-kayt)—to share facts, ideas, or feelings with other people

conversation (kon-vur-SAY-shun)—to talk and listen with someone for a while

extracurricular (ek-struh-kuh-RIK-yoo-ler)—relating to activities that are offered by a school but are not part of the course of study

habit (HAB-it)—something that one does regularly, often without thinking about it

inspire (in-SPYRE)—to fill someone with an emotion, idea, or an attitude

loan (LOHN)—money that is borrowed with a plan to pay it back

motivate (MOH-tuh-vate)—to encourage someone to do something

overwhelm (oh-vur-WELM)—to have a very strong effect

stage fright (STAYJ FRITE)—the nervousness people feel before appearing in front of an audience

READ MORE

Catherman, Jonathan. *The Manual to Middle School: The "Do This, Not That" Survival Guide for Guys*. Grand Rapids, MI: Revell, 2017.

Newman, Catherine. *How to Be a Person: 65 Hugely Useful, Super-Important Skills to Learn before You've Grown Up*. North Adams, MA: Storey Publishing, LLC, 2020.

Sherman, Hannah. *Mindfulness Workbook for Kids: 60+ Activities to Focus, Stay Calm, and Make Good Choices.* Emeryville, CA: Rockridge Press, 2020.

INTERNET SITES

We Are Teachers: 15 Awesome Classroom Activities That Teach Job-Readiness Skills Job Readiness
weareteachers.com/9-awesome-classroom-activities-that-teach-job-readiness-skills

Money Under 30: How To Save Money As A Teen
moneyunder30.com/how-teens-can-save-money

TeensHealth: Organizing Schoolwork & Assignments
kidshealth.org/en/teens/focused.html

INDEX

ABOUT THE AUTHOR

Stephanie Peters has been writing books for young readers for more than 25 years. Among her most recent titles are *Sleeping Beauty: Magic Master* and *Johnny Slimeseed*, both for Capstone's Far-Out Fairy Tales and Folk Tales series. An avid reader, workout enthusiast, and beach wanderer, Stephanie enjoys spending time with her children, Jackson and Chloe, her husband Dan, and the family's two cats and two rabbits. She lives and works in Mansfield, Massachusetts.